T0104129

Buddha Nature

Our Potential for Wisdom, Compassion,
and Happiness

SHAMAR RINPOCHE

Series

Bird
of
Paradise
Press

About Bird of Paradise Press

Bird of Paradise Press is a non-profit book publisher based in the United States. The press specializes in Buddhist meditation and philosophy, as well as other topics from Buddhist perspectives including history, ethics, and governance. Its books are distributed worldwide and available in multiple languages. The bird mentioned in the company's name is said to be from a special place where beings can meet with favorable conditions to progress on their path to awakening.

Also by Shamar Rinpoche

BRINGING MIND TRAINING TO LIFE
An Exploration of the 5th Shamarpa's Concise Lojong Manual

THE PATH TO AWAKENING
How Buddhism's Seven Points of Mind Training Can Lead You to a Life of Enlightenment and Happiness

BOUNDLESS AWAKENING
The Heart of Buddhist Meditation

BOUNDLESS WISDOM
A Mahāmudrā Practice Manual

A GOLDEN SWAN IN TURBULENT WATERS
The Life and Times of the Tenth Karmapa Choying Dorje

THE KING OF PRAYERS
A Commentary on the Noble King of Prayers of Excellent Conduct

CREATING A TRANSPARENT DEMOCRACY
A New Model

BUDDHA NATURE
Our Potential for Wisdom, Compassion, and Happiness

A PATH OF PRACTICE
The Bodhi Path Program

Buddha Nature

Our Potential for Wisdom, Compassion,
and Happiness

SHAMAR RINPOCHE

Translated and introduced by Tina Draszczyk

RABSEL
PUBLICATIONS

Buddha Nature:
Our Potential for Wisdom, Compassion, and Happiness

Copyright © Original Teachings by Shamar Rinpoche, 1988
Copyright © by Bird of Paradise Press, 2019

BIRD OF PARADISE PRESS
Lexington, Virginia, USA
birdofparadisepress.org

Translated and introduced by Tina Draszczyk
Photograph page 20: Thule Jug, 1996

All rights reserved. No part of this book may be reproduced, stored in or introduced in a retrieval system, or transmitted in any form or by any means (electronic, mechanical, photocopying, recording or otherwise) without the prior written permission from the publisher, except for the inclusion of brief quotations in a review or for the private use of readers.

RABSEL PUBLICATIONS
16, rue de Babylone
76430 La Remuée, France
www.rabsel.com
contact@rabsel.com

© Rabsel Éditions, La Remuée, France, 2023
ISBN 978-2-36017-057-9

Table of Contents

1

The nature of sentient beings is always buddhahood.
Not realizing this, they wander endlessly in cyclic existence.
In response to the limitless suffering of sentient beings,
may boundless compassion arise in [our] mind.

3rd Karmapa, Rangjung Dorje
The Mahāmudrā Prayer

Preface
by Jigme Rinpoche

For decades, we were blessed by the teachings transmitted by Shamar Rinpoche in Dhagpo Kagyu Ling, France. In 1988, Rinpoche gave pithy teachings on Buddha Nature in Dhagpo. Rinpoche's words and the topic itself are of true help to the practitioners of the 21st century.

Shamar Rinpoche's words combine the wisdom and experience of the core teachings of the Buddha. Through his modernity, rooted in the meaning of the speech of the Enlightened One, he renders accessible the means to unveil the inner wealth that already lies within each and every one of us to today's practitioners.

Buddha Nature is a central theme for anyone with a sincere wish to journey along the path to actualizing enlightenment. This key notion requires careful consideration so as not to misunderstand it and turn it into another samsaric concept. If correctly understood, this key point will help bring the meditative practice to its fruition. This is exactly what Shamar Rinpoche does with the following teaching: he guides the student to the most fundamental point of each and every sentient being.

Shamar Rinpoche based his explanations on the text called *Revealing Buddha Nature*, a fundamental text within the Karma Kamtsang lineage, written by the 3rd Karmapa, Rangjung Dorje. It is a concise yet precise composition that every serious practitioner should study and get a deep understanding of. On this basis, its meaning should be implemented in one's practice in order for it to bear fruits.

I deeply rejoice that Tina Draszczyk did this wonderful work of editing Shamar Rinpoche's teaching and providing a full translation of the text. This work will be meaningful not only for nowadays practitioners, but for future generations as well. Tina is thus following the footsteps of every genuine practitioner and teacher who makes the Buddha Dharma accessible in an authentic way. I would like to express my gratitude to Tina and all those who helped to complete this work.

With prayers,
Jigme Rinpoche

Dhagpo Kagyu Ling,
September 12th 2018

Preface

by the translator

This book contains the teachings on buddha nature given by the 14th Shamarpa, Mipham Chökyi Lodrö (1952–2014), in Dhagpo Kagyu Ling, France, in the year 1988. In a very inspiring way he clearly pointed to what really counts: the heart of awakening is nothing other than our true nature and therefore all of us, in fact every sentient being, can awaken to his or her buddha qualities.

The Shamarpa based his explanations on the text *Revealing Buddha Nature* composed by the 3rd Karmapa, Rangjung Dorje (1284–1339), which sums up Maitreya/Asaṅga's *Ultimate Continuum*, that is, the *Uttaratantraśāstra,* also known as the *Ratnagotravibhāga*. This latter treatise is considered to reflect the meaning of the so-called third and final cycle of the Buddha's teachings, which is mainly concerned with buddha nature and its qualities.

The first part of this book consists of the Shamarpa's instructions, which at the time were orally translated from the Tibetan by Lama Rinchen, a long-time meditator, translator, and retreat-master, based in France. I would like to thank her wholeheartedly for this great contribution. Based on the original recording, I am offering here a retranslation from the Tibetan and consider it a great privilege to be able to make these pith teachings by the Shamarpa available to a larger audience. The second part of this book presents a translation of *Revealing Buddha Nature* by Karmapa Rangjung Dorje, the text on which these teachings are based.

Moreover, assuming that not all readers are familiar with the Buddhist terms used by Shamar Rinpoche and, in particular, with their specific connotation in the framework of the Karma Kagyu tradition, I thought it might be helpful to add a short explanatory introduction. It is supplemental to the main contents of this book, but is included in case it is helpful to the reader.

My special thanks go to Lara Braitstein, Professor of Buddhist Studies, editor of the Shamarpa's *The Path to Awakening* and co-editor of his *Boundless Wisdom*, as well as to Timothy Riese, both of whom edited the English. I would also like to thank Marjorie Lakin Erickson for additional valuable English-language editing.

I deeply hope that this publication of the 14th Shamarpa's teachings will be of benefit to everyone who comes into contact with it and that it will contribute to the flourishing of the Shamarpas' activities.

Introduction
by the translator

In the recorded teachings that form the basis of this book, Shamar Rinpoche shows that our spiritual path is built on confidence in our true potential, which, in the terminology of Mahāyāna Buddhism, is often referred to as "buddha nature."

Contextualizing buddha nature
In this context, Shamar Rinpoche speaks about the "limitless number of teachings" given by the Buddha in support of Dharma practitioners. From the perspective of Mahāyāna Buddhism, to which Tibetan Buddhism belongs, the Buddha taught in three cycles that are referred to as the three "wheels of Dharma." They are represented in the vast field of sūtras and are further explained in the treatises or śāstras by various Indian Buddhist masters who explain the intent of these sūtras.

Each of the three wheels of Dharma takes a particular focus in order to reveal reality in increasingly profound ways. Whereas the first wheel expounds the Four Noble Truths— that is, the truth of suffering, its origin, its cessation, and the path toward cessation—the second wheel focuses on emptiness—that is, that all outer and inner phenomena lack an inherent self-nature. The third Dharma wheel, often referred to as the one of "precise distinction," carefully distinguishes between existence and nonexistence, being and nonbeing. In this context it is emphasized that, whereas outer and inner phenomena are empty of an inherent self- nature, mind as such—that is, buddha nature—is endowed with the potential of awakening. Naturally, this can be understood in different ways. For some it means that the empty nature of mind provides the room to generate step by step the spiritual qualities that ultimately culminate in the state of buddhahood. For others, it means that the emptiness of mind is primordially imbued with the qualities of awakening; in other words, that mind's true nature here and now is, in fact, the state of awakening. From this perspective, the spiritual path "merely" consists in revealing buddha nature by removing all those obscurations that obstruct an individual from being in touch with his or her actual nature and its qualities. It is exactly this latter view that Shamar Rinpoche presents in this book.

In short, buddha nature is a term that describes the essence of mind. From the perspective of the Kagyu tradition, the only difference between an awakened individual and an ordinary sentient being is that the first has actualized his or her buddha nature, a state referred to as nirvāṇa, while an ordinary sentient being has not actualized his or her buddha nature, a state called saṃsāra or having a "samsaric mind." The difference between nirvāṇa and saṃsāra is therefore just the state of mind. For centuries this has been the guiding principle in the spiritual path as transmitted in the Kagyu tradition. This is evident, for example, in a quote from the 2nd Shamarpa, Khachö Wangpo (1350–1405), who, like the 14th Shamarpa, Mipham Chökyi Lodrö, was a leading master in the Kagyu school as well as its lineage holder:

> In short, this, your present mind—uncontrived, undefiled, unaltered—is itself the heart of all the Victors [i.e., buddha nature]. From the beginning there is nothing to remove and nothing to add. In this regard you should not have the slightest—not the slightest—hope or fear about anything whatsoever. [...] The true nature of the mind in the present is luminosity, immaculate throughout beginningless time. This very nature is called the "genuine nature." Even though it is labeled with hundreds of names [...] it is "just this." It is not established in terms of any objective existence, being by nature the expanse of great emptiness, the actuality of everything, clarity, awareness [and] unobstructedness. It is the appearance of everything. [...] Truly, in this regard, saṃsāra and nirvāṇa, while appearing to be different, are one in nature.[1]

Thus, grounded in the view that mind as such is absolutely healthy, this spiritual path is designed to provide the required conditions for a natural healing process to evolve that heals mind as such from the load of adventitious stains. The concrete starting point for this is the understanding of the common human condition, which brings us back to the Buddha's first wheel of Dharma, the Four Noble Truths. In this regard, a classical Buddhist analogy compares the Buddha with a physician who first diagnoses the disease of a patient, then continues to explore and describe the cause(s) of the ailment, then offers to the patient the prospect of regaining his or her health, and finally advises what is to be done in order to reach this aim, providing the details of the treatment, which allows for the healing process to work.

The truth of suffering, its origin, its cessation, and the path toward cessation

In this vein, the Buddha's diagnosis regarding the life of ordinary sentient beings is that it is a state of suffering. "Duḥkha," the original Sanskrit term for what in English is often rendered as "suffering," has various implications; among others it covers subtle and coarse tension, dissatisfaction, stress, and physical as well as psychological pain, big and small. Along with this diagnosis, the Buddha encouraged his students not to ignore this situation or smooth it over, but instead to turn toward it. He advised that one should make an effort to deeply understand this basic situation. He then continued to point out its origin, explaining that the origin of suffering lies in one's unawareness of reality, automatic mental impulses, and the clinging and rejecting that go along with them. He admonished his students to make efforts to overcome the origin of suffering. To encourage practitioners in this endeavor, the Buddha pointed out that it is possible to achieve freedom from suffering and ultimate happiness, the cessation of suffering. Yet, it does not happen on its own. One needs to practice a path toward this aim.

The samsaric cycle of existence

As long as an individual does not make an effort to overcome the origin of suffering, he or she will continue to live in a state of mind that, as described above, is of a samsaric nature with its infinite loops of tension, dissatisfaction, and pain. This, in Buddhist terms, is referred to as the "samsaric cycle of existence." This term implies that these loops are not limited to this very life at present, but that exactly the same patterns have been going on in the past, in previous lives, and—unless removed—will continue in future lives. From the Buddhist perspective these lives can take on all kinds of shapes, in pleasant, mixed, and very unpleasant surroundings. It is explained that intentional acts leave karmic imprints or seeds in the samsaric mind that, as they come to ripen, so to speak *propel* the individual into environments that mirror these intentions and actions. On the face of it, this seems to describe a situation in which sentient beings are born into different types of external worlds. Moreover, from the samsaric individual's perspective the world one lives in is certainly experienced as a real world, just as we know this from our present human existence. However, when explored from the perspective of Mahāyāna Buddhism, what appears as if it were an outer world is explained to be but a projection of the samsaric mind and its delusions.

There is no external world

In this regard, the Shamarpa says "nothing we perceive is anything other than the confused appearances of a confused mind." To find access to this intricate statement it might be helpful to start with what is obvious and what the Buddha presented in the truth of suffering: everything is impermanent. Impermanence in turn has many layers from coarse to subtle. While everyone knows that the seasons change and that gross things such as a house or the body at a certain point in time collapse or die, the more subtle level of impermanence easily escapes our attention. In fact, impermanence happens at every moment. Its most subtle level is that, as a moment comes into being, it is already in a process of change. And so it is impossible to identify a moment in which something actually abides and thus truly exists in its own right, independently of something else.

This brings us to the second wheel of Dharma, in which the Buddha taught that, for this very reason, phenomena lack a true self-nature. Whereas phenomena appear, manifest, and function, these are just processes of change. Not for a split second is there anything static or abiding. In accordance with these Buddhist teachings, as far as outer phenomena are concerned, quantum physicists came to the conclusion that the world we perceive is not an objective fact, but merely a dynamic flux of interactions. From this perspective, the Buddhist teachings are not very different. Because the world one perceives is not an objective fact, the perception of it cannot be anything else than a subjective process. And this brings us to the perceiving mind. If the seemingly perceived world does not truly exist even for a split second, the perception of it as a seemingly consistent and ongoing reality must take place in the constructing or, in Buddhist terms, samsaric mind. This understanding makes it easier to relate to the Buddhist notion of the cycle of rebirths. In addition, it puts the entire effort of striving for a spiritual path into place: as it is one's own samsaric mind that constructs and projects, one can (and in fact should) take the responsibility of training one's mind in ways that lead to freedom and well-being. It is in this regard that Shamar Rinpoche here emphasizes training in "bodhicitta" as the paramount way to do so. Let us look then at this notion of bodhicitta, which is *the* essential practice in Mahāyāna Buddhism.

Bodhicitta
Even though there are a number of translations for bodhicitta such as "enlightened mind," "mind of awakening," etc., it is not easy to find a to-the-point translation in English. Let us therefore have a quick glance at the Sanskrit term itself: "bodhi" means "being awakened" and designates the state of a buddha. In fact, "buddha" is connected with this term. "Citta," the second part of the word, means "mind" and is about focusing one's heart and mind fully on "bodhi." This is done on various levels, which are traditionally divided into relative and ultimate bodhicitta. The first lies within our conventions, that is, our thoughts, intentions, and concrete ways of acting. This is why the translation "conventional bodhicitta" would fit as well. Ultimate bodhicitta refers to the non-dual state of being awakened that the intellect cannot fathom.

In Mahāyāna Buddhism, relative or conventional bodhicitta is further subdivided into aspiration and application bodhicitta. The former means to faithfully strive for the awakened state of a buddha— to become free from obstructions, delusions, and suffering. The latter, bodhicitta of application, means to actually and continually take those steps in the context of ethics, meditation, and view that lead toward ultimate awakening ("bodhi"). *The* crucial perspective of both bodhicitta of aspiration and of application is that one does not just wish for one's own well- being but for that of all sentient beings. Along with focusing on one's own spiritual path, bodhicitta thus pertains to the altruistic, compassionate, and heartfelt wish ("citta") to support others. An important basis for this motivation is to understand that oneself and all other sentient beings share the common situation of suffering because of karma and mental afflictions. This situation holds true for the same and very simple reason as outlined above already: we are not aware of our minds' true nature. Yet, these afflictions, delusions, and all their consequences are but adventitious and fleeting. Instead of being part of mind's true nature, they merely conceal it. Every sentient being could let go of these afflictions and their effects—simply because they are insubstantial and unreal. The afflictions operate only due to the lack of awareness of mind's actual nature. From the Mahāyāna perspective, it is essential to understand that this common situation is shared by everyone and to see that every sentient being has the potential for awakening even if, on a mere surface level, this potential might hardly be evident. In short, relative bodhicitta means wishing to support and actually supporting all sentient beings—and this naturally also includes oneself—so that access to wisdom, happiness, and loving kindness, that is, to buddhahood, becomes possible. Ultimate bodhicitta designates the awakened mind ("citta") that, free from all obscurations, is aware of its true nature ("bodhi"). It is called "ultimate" or "absolute" because it is not dual and is beyond all conditioning. In this sense ultimate bodhicitta is not different from buddha nature. The path toward its realization is to generate relative bodhicitta and to cultivate a view that corresponds to ultimate bodhicitta. On the one hand ultimate bodhicitta is thus the fruition. On the other hand, it is mind's true nature here and now. In this way, the path nurtures the unfolding of that which has always been one's true nature. Those who proceed on their spiritual path with bodhicitta are called bodhisattvas and the realization that will be accomplished is perfect buddhahood. In this book, Shamar Rinpoche's advice to focus on bodhicitta has, first of all, to do with relative bodhicitta. At the same time, however, as will become evident on the pages to come, he gives these teachings from a bird's eye view of ultimate bodhicitta.

The wisdom of buddhahood: the dharmakāya and the form-kāyas

The last part in this introduction concerns the so-called "kāya," a term that will also appear frequently in this book. Again, as it is difficult to render "kāya" properly inEnglish, the Sanskrit terms will be utilized throughout this book. Literally, "kāya" means "body" or "embodiment." It also has the connotation of something rich and complex. In the present context, "kāya" is used to describe the qualities of the state of awakening; that is, the wisdom and compassion of buddhahood. In this regard and in describing its various qualities, in the Mahāyāna there is the classical two-fold distinction between the "dharmakāya" and the "form kāyas."

The "dharmakāya" designates mind's ultimate nature and might thus be rendered as the "embodiment of reality" or as "the embodiment of enlightened qualities," in that *dharma* in this context, and from the Kagyus' perspective, means both. In this sense, the dharmakāya mainly concerns the state of ultimate well-being; of buddhahood as such.

The "form kāyas" are the manifestations of awakening that benefit others. A distinction is made between the so- called "sambhogakāya" and "nirmāṇakāya," a distinction that concerns the ways in which the state of awakening is helpful for others. "Sambhogakāya" literally means the "embodiment of enjoyment." It is said to consist in very subtle physical appearances that are perceptible only by individuals with a pure mind; in other words, by realized bodhisattvas. The "enjoyment" refers to the great wealth and abundance of the Mahāyāna, in that the environment of such manifestations is pure, the company is pure, the Dharma being taught is pure, etc. As this purity is not shared by sentient beings with their samsaric mind that is contaminated by ignorance, ordinary individuals are not capable of relating to the sambhogakāya. Yet, they are able to interact with the second type of form kāya, called nirmāṇakāya. "Nirmāṇakāya" can be rendered as the "embodiment of emanations." The type of manifestation meant here is on a coarser level, such as a human body. The nirmāṇakāya was best exemplified by Buddha Śākyamuni who lived about 2500 years ago and benefited others by instructing them on the path of Dharma.

In this book, Shamar Rinpoche examines all these qualities of buddha wisdom, pointing out that— as mentioned above—buddhahood is inherent to the mind. He thus reveals buddha nature with its qualities as the core being of each of us.

I hope that this short foray into some basic principles of Buddhism in general, and Mahāyāna Buddhism in particular, serves as helpful background information for the pages to follow.

Vienna, Austria
October 24, 2018

The 14th Shamarpa

Buddha Nature

Our Potential for Wisdom, Compassion, and Happiness

as taught by the 14th Shamarpa Mipham Chökyi Lodrö, based on the 3rd Karmapa, Rangjung Dorje's *Revealing Buddha Nature*

Ignorance does not have a concrete beginning, but it does have an end

The Buddha gave a limitless number of teachings to correspond to the limitless challenges sentient beings are faced with. All of them are designed to support practitioners in the endeavor to realize their buddha nature, mind's true mode of being.

The word "mind" covers two basic aspects. On the one hand it denotes the samsaric mind, and on the other hand it refers to the true nature of mind.

Among the many issues with our samsaric mind, the root problem is ignorance. Ignorance is like an ever-present veil of unawareness that triggers all our problems. We may compare this with the effect of a chronic heart disease: in the same way that a chronic heart condition that limits the functioning of the heart will result in oxygen not circulating properly and therefore affect the body as a whole, the obscuration that is our mind's ignorance is the root source of all of our problems.

What is this ignorance? Simply put, it means that in each and every moment the mind is not fully aware of its true nature. In other words, the mind as such does not know itself and therefore remains in a state of ignorance. In this state of unawareness, all kinds of concepts, thoughts, and emotions evolve that influence our actions as a consequence of which we wander around in the samsaric cycle of existence, with all its illusions and confusion.

The samsaric mind is confused in the sense that it is in a state of constant distraction because of not abiding in its true nature. The specific function or character of the mind is to know and to experience. When the mind is distracted, this knowing or experiencing is turned outward instead of toward itself. The mind relates to what seems to be an external world by perceiving phenomena such as sensations that occur based on the body's sense organs. For example, through the medium of the eye-consciousness, the mind is distracted by the visual forms it beholds. Through the medium of the ear-consciousness, it is distracted by the sounds that are heard, and so on. Based on these perceptions and their associated sensations, the mind makes distinctions and evaluates what is being perceived as good or bad, pleasant or unpleasant, etc. These distinctions solidify into the further distractions of attachment and aversion, and fix the mind in a purely dualistic framework. This process of distraction is driven further by the forces of mental afflictions and emotions. Their intense and at times aggressive nature colors the distraction, and turns it into something that is not wholesome.

Consequently, reactive patterns of feeling and acting that reflect these conditioned distinctions occur. All this happens in the samsaric mind that has ignorance as its basic pattern. If the mind could behold its own true nature, it would not be under the sway of dualistic delusion, but experience reality as it is. However, as the mind is not aware of its own nature, its ongoing natural capacity to know and experience is thus externalized in the form of the distractions described above.

In this way, nothing we perceive is anything other than the confused appearance of a confused mind.

You might assume that all of this must have started at a specific point in time. However, there is no identifiable beginning to ignorance and its associated samsaric states of mind. We can compare this to having a dream about a horse. Ask yourself whether the horse in your dream has a real beginning. The answer to this question is "no" for the reason that the horse is just a dream image and therefore does not truly exist. Thus, the horse did not truly come into being at a certain point in time; it is just the confused projection of a confused mind, experienced as if it were real. The moment you awake, the horse is no longer there. The mind has stopped projecting the horse, due to which the perception of the horse has come to an end. In exactly this way it can be said that even though there is no concrete beginning to delusion, there is an end. Likewise, deluded samsaric perceptions don't have a concrete beginning, but they can have an end: the state of awakening.

Another question may arise. We might wonder how, if the true nature of the mind is free from delusion, did it become confused? Where did this ignorance come from? This doubt might linger in your mind, but for beginners on the path it is not very helpful to brood over this question too much.[2] In the course of meditation practice the answer will become clear.

As the delusions are cleared away, mind's true nature— buddha nature—reveals itself and appears as the inconceivable wisdom of buddhahood. At the moment we are not capable of fathoming this state of mind, simply due to the fact that, as ordinary sentient beings, we are limited by our deluded dualistic states of mind to the extent that a capacity to grasp the undeluded wisdom of enlightenment is beyond our reach. Nevertheless, analogies are provided, as well as descriptions, so that we can somehow relate to the state of awakening.

Scriptural sources

Descriptions of buddha nature are found mainly in the sūtras that, from the Mahāyāna perspective, are said to make up the third cycle of the Buddha's teachings, and in the associated explanatory teachings. In these sources, the qualities of buddha nature and the state of buddhahood are elucidated in detail. Among the explanatory works, the *Uttaratantraśāstra* or the *Teaching of the Ultimate Continuum* goes into the greatest detail. Based on these explanations and summarizing the main points, the 3rd Karmapa, Rangjung Dorje, composed his works *Distinguishing Wisdom and Consciousness* and *Revealing Buddha Nature*.

Mind, the foundation of everything

In Buddhist philosophy, mind is sometimes referred to as the ground (Sanskrit: ālaya), or the foundation of everything. It is considered the basis of all the deluded processes of wandering in cyclic existence as well as of the attainment of buddhahood in that all enlightened qualities manifest on the basis of mind once delusion is removed. In short, we may describe it in such a way that there are two aspects: the deluded aspect, and the aspect of freedom from delusion. Both are inseparable from mind.

In the state of delusion we cling to a self, based on our experience of the ground consciousness, a process that is called the defiled mind. Self-clinging continues to operate through the medium of the six types of consciousness: the sense of sight, the sense of sound, the sense of smell, the sense of taste, the sense of touch, and the sense of mind. The "sense of mind" primarily perceives the movements of thoughts, concepts, and emotions in the samsaric mind. All in all, we may therefore distinguish eight aspects of the samsaric mind: the ground consciousness, the defiled mind (self-clinging), and the six types of sense-consciousness. As a consequence of self-clinging, the strong afflictions of desire, anger, ignorance, pride, and jealousy arise. Then, based on these afflictions, the samsaric mind produces all kinds of thoughts, concepts, and emotions. It produces millions of them, thus maintaining the mind's samsaric mode. This is how the confused mind operates.

The aspect of mind free of delusion operates when mind's workings are purified. At that time, the ground reveals itself as the wisdom of buddhahood, manifesting as the state of omniscience. When the clinging to an "I" and a "mine" is removed, the afflictions cease to occur. What is left at that point is thus undeluded knowing, perfect enlightened wisdom, the realization of buddha nature.

You may wonder how the deluded aspect of the ground consciousness transforms into a mind of wisdom. The answer is that there is no real change involved. Instead, what happens is that the removal of delusion and deluded perceptions makes mind—as it truly is—evident. The samsaric mind is a state in which the ground may be said to be ill, in a state of psychological disorder caused by delusion. It is these impurities that are removed progressively on the spiritual path.

The most intense impurities that prevent us from seeing mind's true nature are the afflictions induced by clinging to the self, where we identify with the ground consciousness as our own continuous identity.

This pattern has been ongoing since beginningless time. And when we are under the sway of this self-clinging, further afflictions arise naturally and these motivate actions. When we act, traces of the physical, verbal, and mental deeds are stored in the ground consciousness. This process thus perpetuates itself. I will use an analogy to illustrate. When the earth is moistened by rain, more humidity is released into the air. This in turn leads to more rain falling on the earth, leading to a continuous cycle of rain, condensation, and more rain. Likewise, self-clinging and the associated afflictions trigger actions of body, speech, and mind. These actions cause us to accumulate karma and the habitual tendencies thus accrued gather in the ground consciousness. They later ripen, leading to further afflictions and further karma-producing actions. It is through this process that the deluded perceptions of the cycle of samsaric existences continue.

Unless you purify yourself of afflictions and karma, you will not be capable of seeing that the true nature of mind is wisdom. Even if—in meditation, for example—you try to look at the true nature of mind, your afflictions and karmic workings prevent you from recognizing its nature. This is because before the fruition of seeing mind's true nature can mature, other latent karmic tendencies ripen and obstruct this process. They hinder or damage your capacity to see that mind's true nature is the buddha mind. To illustrate this with an example, let's say you wish to cross an ocean by boat. If the boat is damaged before you reach the other shore, you cannot arrive at your desired destination. Likewise, before you reach the result of realizing the nature of mind as buddha wisdom, other karmic seeds ripen and prevent this process. Your "boat" is damaged, and you cannot reach the other shore. It is therefore essential to purify the mind of afflictive and karmic obscurations first. Without this first step, it is not possible to succeed in the realization of mind's true nature.

Begin with bodhicitta

In order to accomplish the realization of mind's true nature, to actualize the state of awakening, there are two things we need to do. First, we have to purify ourselves of the negative mental tendencies that are due to afflictions and negative karmic actions. Second, we need to engage in virtuous actions, which create the causes for the blossoming of enlightened qualities. The method to ensure this happens is to generate bodhicitta.[3] In Mahāyāna Buddhism, therefore, we develop and cultivate bodhicitta from the very beginning of the path until the state of awakening is attained. It might usefully be compared to a railway track that a train follows until it reaches the desired destination. Similarly, on the track of bodhicitta, spiritual development leads to the realization of buddhahood. This is why, in Mahāyāna scriptures, generating bodhicitta is always emphasized at the beginning of a practice. It must be generated before we engage in any particular method. It is thus the main cause for a practitioner's attainment of buddhahood.

The afflictions are rooted in self-clinging, but bodhicitta is rooted in the concern for the well-being of others. In this sense, bodhicitta on the one hand, and afflictions, as well as the karmic tendencies stored in the ground consciousness on the other hand, are opposites. That is why bodhicitta has the power to eliminate all negativities or hindrances, to counteract the afflictions and karmic tendencies. On the basis of bodhicitta, whatever we do in terms of both attitudes and actions becomes positive, as it is directed toward other beings' welfare. Therefore, instead of working for your own benefit, if you generate the remedy of bodhicitta in the very beginning, from the very start of your spiritual journey all of your actions will be oriented toward the benefit of others and thereby become continuously meritorious. This is how we develop. Thus, with bodhicitta we acquire the antidote to afflictions and negative karmic actions.

Right from the beginning, the power of bodhicitta's virtue suppresses the power of negative karma and prevents negative karmic seeds from ripening. This means that you will find yourself in better circumstances, with better opportunities to proceed on the path toward realization. On this basis, whatever specific method you apply in your endeavor to achieve buddhahood will be successful. Further cultivation of bodhicitta will finally enable you to completely eradicate all afflictions, karma, and obscurations. That means that you will attain the state of a buddha. The generation of bodhicitta is the main cause for this development in the Mahāyāna designed to bring us to full awakening. The practitioner is therefore recommended to give rise to bodhicitta first, and to engage in the various practices on this basis. Generating bodhicitta first ensures that you will be able to proceed all the way to buddhahood.

The main topic of this treatise is the wisdom of buddhahood, which is the result we need to attain. This very result is found in each and everyone's mind, in our buddha nature. Yet, we cannot attain buddhahood on the spot. It does not happen immediately. To actualize our inherent buddha nature we need to follow a path that will make the wisdom of our mind manifest. We need to work with our present deluded state, and we have to do this with bodhicitta. This can be done in two equally excellent ways, and the one you choose depends entirely on your own motivation. They both lead to the same result.

The first way is performing virtuous actions with the motivation that in future lives we will be better able to help others, to support them on a larger scale than we are able to in this life. In this sense we may say that our intention is to attain better rebirths in saṃsāra. Actions performed with this intention are very powerful. The karmic result of virtuous actions coupled with this intention is that in our next rebirth we will naturally find ourselves in circumstances where we are of benefit to others. It is not that we will consciously remember that we wanted to be of help to others. Rather, the ability to help others will occur naturally as a karmic result. Since in that future lifetime we are naturally better able to benefit others, the fruit of our positive actions becomes even greater, which means that in further rebirths we will be reborn in circumstances where we will be able to benefit others even more. This process continues in such a way that we progress toward awakening as we attain rebirth after rebirth, each time more and more effectively helping others and performing virtuous actions. Eventually, this leads to the state of buddhahood. If we wish to take rebirth again and again in order to benefit sentient beings, we must understand that this will come about through the power of virtuous actions. If this isn't clear, we risk rebirth in the lower realms of saṃsāra. As we do not remember our previous lives, we cannot know that we prepared ourselves to proceed on the spiritual path in this manner. It is only through the power of the meritorious karma accumulated by performing virtuous deeds that our life will naturally take this turn. If we know how to proceed this way, this approach toward attaining buddhahood is excellent.[4]

The second way is based on the intention to achieve buddhahood in this very lifetime in order to accomplish the benefit of others in an immense way. To follow this way, we therefore search for powerful methods to purify ourselves of all the karma and afflictions that we experience at present. The essential means for accomplishing that aim is genuine compassion. If we have genuine, non-artificial compassion, we can within this very lifetime clear away the karmic potential of all previous negative actions as well as the veils and impurities that obstruct our mind. Through this purification based on true compassion for all sentient beings we can attain the state of buddhahood in this lifetime. As with the other approach, we must thoroughly understand the method for proceeding in this way. With that clear understanding, this path is an equally excellent way of achieving enlightenment.[5]

Both approaches will bring about the same result, and both correspond with the great vehicle. In both cases it is essential to accumulate merit, i.e., to generate virtuous intentions and engage in wholesome deeds, because this is what makes the realization of the result of buddhahood possible. In *Revealing Buddha Nature*, Karmapa Rangjung Dorje mainly speaks about this result, encouraging us to strive for its realization.

Buddha wisdom,
the true nature of mind

The wisdom of a buddha is present as a potential within our mind. In fact, our mind is essentially permeated by buddha wisdom, just as peanuts, for example, are permeated by oil. We arrive at this essence of the mind when we clear our mind of all impurities. This allows for mind's wisdom to expand, in other words, for the realization of buddhahood.

The wisdom of buddhahood is expressed as two qualities: the dharmakāya and the form kāyas. In brief, the dharmakāya is the realization of mind's true nature and the form kāyas are physical manifestations through which our true nature benefits others.

The thirty-two qualities of the dharmakāya

The thirty-two qualities of the dharmakāya are subdivided into three sections: the ten powers, the four types of fearlessness, and the eighteen qualities exclusive to buddhas.

The ten powers
(qualities 1–10)

The first set of the dharmakāya's qualities is known as the ten powers. "Power" in this context refers to the capacity for limitless knowledge.

(1) The first aspect of a buddha's knowledge is referred to as "knowledge of what is a basis and what is not a basis." It pertains to knowing in detail how virtuous and non- virtuous deeds come to ripen. A buddha knows that based on virtue, wholesome results come about, and that based on non-virtue, unwholesome results are produced. Non-virtue is therefore not a basis for pleasant results. This way of knowing is not meant in a common sense, the way one may understand, for example, that protecting the life of sentient beings will bring about positive results, and that damaging them will bring about negative ones. Even as ordinary human beings we can broadly understand that doing something positive will lead to a positive result and that negative actions will bring about negative results. As a power of awakening, this knowledge means much more. It is about precise knowledge of this pattern. The thoughts of ordinary sentient beings occur in an unending way. If we can transform our mental activity in a virtuous direction, there will be endless virtuous thoughts. Likewise, when we have a negative attitude, this condition turns the unending mental activities into unending negative or non-virtuous concepts. And just as positive and negative

thoughts are without any limits, likewise the ways in which these come to ripen as karmic results are without any limit. Only a buddha has the capacity to know each and every detail of these complex processes. For example, if one plants the small seed of a tree, the result of its ripening will be a huge tree with a big trunk, a great number of branches, and the carrying of a large quantity of leaves and fruits. In addition, the tree will remain for only a certain period of time. To know all of the details of the ways in which a single seed will come to ripen is extremely difficult. This it is the first of the ten powers.

(2) The second power pertains to knowledge of karmic actions and their fruits. It is the capacity to be directly aware of what causes were accumulated in the past to produce a situation in the present, a specific karmic result. For example, it includes the power to know what kind of karmic causes were responsible for an individual's rebirth as a human with his or her individual personality. It means to directly and unmistakenly know in detail what the positive and negative karmic causes were for a specific present result.

(3) The third power is to know the nature of the variety of sentient beings. Modern science does confirm some of these Buddhist notions, such as the view that there are a countless number of different galaxies. "Sentient being" simply means to be endowed with a mind, which pertains to the capacity to experience, know, and feel. It is through this ability that a being perceives and

relates to his or her environment. Most people are accustomed to concerning themselves with the material world, the inanimate aspect of life, but don't have a very good understanding of mind and its workings. We tend to assume that any creature that shows intelligence is a sentient being that has a mind, but we don't generally assume the same thing for very small creatures. For example, we are quite willing to agree that large beings such as elephants, whales, or dolphins have a mind. We consider a dolphin to be cute and intelligent and thus attribute a mind to it. On the other hand, for many people it might be difficult to imagine that a mosquito has a mind. But every sentient being has a mind, regardless of its size. From the Buddhist perspective there are countless worlds and accordingly there are countless sentient beings of different types. The third power consists of the detailed knowledge of the limitless number, nature, and different characters of sentient beings.

(4) The fourth power is to be aware of the capacities of sentient beings. This refers to understanding sentient beings' abilities to progress on the path toward liberation, each according to his or her capacity. With this power, a buddha is able to see whether or not certain people are able to immediately follow a path designed to benefit others. If not, the capacity of this being is considered to be inferior, and accordingly, the Buddha taught an approach that is appropriate for this person. For those who have the motivation to attain buddhahood for the benefit

of all beings, he taught the Mahāyāna Dharma. Sentient beings are limitless, and each has particular faculties or abilities that are therefore endless in variety as well. In response, the Buddha taught the Dharma in all its diversity.

(5) The fifth power is knowledge of the manifold intentions of sentient beings. A buddha knows each and every intention of everyone in detail. Intention and capacity are quite different. What a sentient being is capable of doing is his or her capacity, whereas the intention is what he or she thinks of doing or intends to do. The intentions that a buddha knows are not only common intentions—for example, that somebody intends to do a certain practice, such as taking the initiation of Amitābha and engaging in the corresponding meditation. A buddha also understands the deeper intentions that beings are themselves sometimes not aware of. Only when certain conditions come together do sentient beings become conscious of these subtle states of mind in which case they are also more successful in accomplishing a particular practice or teaching. A buddha's knowledge in this regard is limitless.

(6) The sixth power is knowledge of the vehicles. Because sentient beings have all kinds of capacities and intentions, the Buddha taught many different types of vehicles or yānas. This means that there are numerous ways to approach enlightenment. The Buddha taught an endless number of yānas to suit the different capacities and intentions of sentient beings, and after his

lifetime the great Indian masters and paṇḍitas systematized all these approaches into the three yānas: the Śrāvakayāna, Pratyekabuddhayāna and Bodhisattvayāna. These three yānas therefore cover all of the Buddha's teachings. In spite of the existence of this system, there is actually no limit to the yānas. There can be any number of yānas, corresponding to the great variety of concepts in sentient beings' minds. A buddha has the power to know the capacities and intentions of sentient beings, and therefore knows what kind of path or vehicle to teach to each sentient being.

(7) The seventh power is the knowledge of meditation and of the meditative absorptions of sentient beings. Also included in this power is knowledge of the afflictions of sentient beings. This enables a buddha to know both how the meditative states of sentient beings are affected by afflictions, as well as what pure meditative states unaffected by afflictions are like. As someone meditates, one begins on the path of accumulation and gradually progresses to higher levels. From the path of accumulation one proceeds to the path of preparation, from there to the paths of vision and cultivation, and finally to the path of no-more-learning. Throughout this process there are particular types of samādhi states; that is, meditative absorptions, meditative experiences, and realizations associated with each path. An ordinary person who is on the small path of accumulation, for example, can only slightly distinguish between the medi-

tative absorption of calm abiding (śamatha) and of deep insight (vipaśyanā). And as for the path of vision, for example, the state of meditative absorption attained is completely inconceivable for an ordinary person. It is only a buddha's unobstructed omniscient wisdom that precisely knows these types of meditative absorptions.

(8) The eighth power or knowledge is the supernatural capacity of what is called "the divine eye." It is a superior kind of vision, one that is bent on benefiting others. With his or her divine eye, a buddha knows in detail the moment and place of death and birth of each and every individual sentient being.

(9) The ninth power is to fully recollect previous rebirths. In an unobstructed and limitless way a buddha sees the whole process of each and every action performed throughout previous lives since beginningless time. This knowledge pertains both to the previous lives of all sentient beings as well as to those of the buddha himself. This knowledge should not be confused with the general type of heightened perception that some people have. A buddha's knowledge is something entirely different from that, because a buddha knows everything in detail.

(10) The tenth power is peace, and refers to the knowledge that all defilements—even the subtlest ones—have come to an end. The powers one through nine are already extremely difficult to attain, but this tenth power, being so subtle, is the most difficult of all. It is the state of com-

plete purification of all impurities. No one but a buddha has this knowledge, because this total purification is attained only with the state of absolute enlightenment.

We cannot truly understand the qualities of enlightenment, as they are beyond the reach of dualistic perception. Therefore, even though these ten powers have been described, we cannot fully know what the state of mind and knowledge of a buddha are like.

The four types of fearlessness
(qualities 11–14)

By virtue of these ten powers, a buddha is endowed with four types of fearlessness. The term "fear" as it is used here does not refer to our common understanding of it as a sense of anxiety. Instead, it refers to the fact that a buddha does not have any hesitations.

(11) The first fearlessness is the freedom from hesitation to proclaim, "I am a buddha." For example, Buddha Śākyamuni had no hesitation to proclaim, "I am a buddha," as he was himself the proof of it. Unless one has achieved the state of awakening, one cannot prove that this is the case. Therefore, a person who has not attained complete enlightenment does not dare say, "I am a buddha." Buddha Śākyamuni could prove that he is enlightened because of having attained the state of a buddha.

(12) The second fearlessness is the freedom from hesitation to point out the obstacles to liberation. A

buddha points out the obstacles of desire, anger, ignorance, jealousy, pride, etc. He is not insecure that this might not be the case. He does not hesitate to communicate his own understanding because he has realized this truth.

In the early days in India, someone invented a tradition that purported to summarize the methods of liberation from the illusion of saṃsāra and attainment of nirvāṇa in six sentences. In fact, the founder of this tradition had the selfish intention of attracting a great number of followers in order to control them with his teachings. This tradition was called "the owl's descendant." When he was questioned on the authenticity and effectiveness of his six sentences, he answered that the six phrases had been given to him by the gods. When he was pressed to explain what made him so certain, he told the following story: One day an emanation of the gods in the form of an owl seated itself at his window. He asked the owl about the six sentences, and the owl nodded in approval of each. He gave this as the proof that his teaching was authentic. This kind of person does not have the fearlessness or freedom from hesitation in terms of the teaching he is providing. Who would believe an owl? The Buddha's teaching is not like this at all. It can be proven to be authentic.

The point is that if you are teaching a path to liberation from saṃsāra, you must fully understand all of the mistakes that can be made on this path from the beginning to the end. If you have this knowledge, you will not hesitate to point out the authentic path to others. If you don't have this knowledge, you should have hesitations, because in this case you will mislead others. By virtue of their complete knowledge, buddhas don't need to have such hesitations.

(13) The third fearlessness is freedom from hesitation to teach the Dharma in order to free sentient beings from saṃsāra, the path with its methods. A buddha unhesitatingly shows the right path using the right methods to guide students toward enlightenment. For example, when Marpa (1012–1097), one of the main Tibetan forefathers of the Kagyu lineage, was teaching Milarepa (1040–1123), who was to become one of the greatest yogis Tibet has ever witnessed, he first put him through a series of hardships. He made him construct a tower four consecutive times in shapes that corresponded to the four types of activities: pacifying, increasing, powerful, and wrathful. Every time he built one, Marpa told Milarepa to tear it down again, only to order him to build a new one. Marpa repeated this four times. Marpa applied this method in order to prepare Milarepa for the teachings. If one does not know that this exact method is helpful for the student in question, one cannot apply this method. It would be too risky, and make the disciple go through experiences that are not conducive to the path. At the time, Milarepa needed this kind of process. But there is no certainty that this approach is suitable for others. By virtue of this fearlessness, a buddha has no hesitation regarding what guidance is

required at which time for which student, and correspondingly points out the methods of the path.

(14) The fourth freedom from hesitation concerns the result. When a teacher is teaching a student, for example, he or she must have the confidence that the path along which he or she is guiding the student leads to the fruit of awakening, to buddhahood. Otherwise, the teacher might mislead the student. In fact it is only a buddha, free from all hesitations, who has the capacity to know that following this path in this way will bring about buddhahood, and who can state that the students he or she has supported on the path have attained enlightenment.

While the first and second fearlessness pertain to the freedom from hesitation regarding a buddha's attainment of awakening and what obstructs such realization, the third and fourth fearlessnesses consist of freedom from hesitation regarding the path and the result.

The eighteen qualities exclusive to buddhas

By virtue of the four types of fearlessness, buddhas have eighteen qualities that are unique when compared to śrāvaka- and pratyekabuddha-arhats as well as to bodhisattvas. These qualities are superior to those of arhats and bodhisattvas. They are therefore described as qualities exclusive to the buddhas.

[*The eighteen qualities exclusive to buddhas are subdivided into four sections. The first six refer to their behavior in body, speech, and mind, and their absolutely flawless way of training other sentient beings. The subsequent six pertain to the realization of buddhas, the next three to buddhas' activities, and the last three of the eighteen to the qualities of their wisdom.*]

Behavior and way of training sentient beings (qualities 15–20)

(15) A buddha's physical behavior is, first of all, always perfect. This is because it is completely free of delusion. In other words, from one perspective, the conduct of śrāvaka- and pratyeka-buddha-arhats and of bodhisattvas, compared to the physical conduct of ordinary beings, is pure. However, compared to that of a buddha, it is not absolutely perfect.

(16) The second quality refers to a buddha's speech. When teaching the Dharma, a buddha never engages in idle chatter, and never speaks inappropriately or incorrectly. Śrāvaka- and pratyeka-buddha-arhats and bodhisattvas also use their speech correctly when teaching the Dharma, but compared with a buddha, their speech is not entirely pure. As long as a being has not attained the perfect state of a buddha, there will be times when the being's speech is not absolutely perfect.

(17) The third quality refers to a buddha's mind. A buddha has a complete, unhindered recollection of everything. The śrāvaka- and pratyekabud-

dha-arhats and bodhisattvas have very good memories, but they are not complete and unhindered. The pratyekabuddha-arhats' memory exceeds that of śrāvaka-arhats. And the bodhisattvas' memory exceeds that of pratyekabuddha-arhats. But they all have moments where they cannot perfectly recollect the past. Only a buddha has the full and unhindered capacity to remember everything.

(18) The fourth quality concerns the state of meditative absorption. In all of the four possible types of activities— walking, moving around, lying, and sitting—a buddha is always in meditative absorption. In comparison, a realized bodhisattva can remain for a long period of time in meditative absorption, but there are also times during post-meditation when he or she is not in meditation. As for śrāvaka- and pratyekabuddha-arhats, there are times during their lives when they do not meditate. Once they leave this life and abide in the state without remainder,[6] they are constantly in a state of meditative absorption; however, this is not the fully perfected or ultimate meditative absorption. Only buddhas abide in the ultimate meditative absorption. There is never a moment when they waver from it.

(19) The fifth of the eighteen qualities exclusive to a buddha is that a buddha never entertains the concept that cyclic existence and the state of buddhahood (nirvāṇa) are different from each other. A buddha does not split these two apart. A buddha fully knows the true nature of ev-

erything, and knows that saṃsāra and nirvāṇa are not different. From our own unenlightened point of view, saṃsāra and nirvāṇa are different. For us this distinction is normal and in fact required; otherwise, we confuse ourselves.

(20) The sixth of the eighteen qualities is freedom from lack of discernment. A buddha always accurately discerns exactly what is required by whom and is therefore never in a state of lacking discernment. On the other hand, it can happen that arhats and bodhisattvas are not aware of what kind of guidance will benefit a specific sentient being. The following illustrates an example. The great Arhat Kāśyapa, one of the very close disciples of the Buddha, was once approached by Devadatta who requested that Kāśyapa teach him the skill of miracles. Kāśyapa was not able at that time to discern Devadatta's intentions, and taught him this skill. But Devadatta had made this request for teachings in order to put an evil plan into effect, and with the skill of performing miracles, he created great problems. When he first approached Kāśyapa, Devadatta pretended to be truly devoted to the Buddha and to be a perfect practitioner. In fact, the ability to perform miracles has nothing to do with spiritual realization. This ability is rather based on the capacity to focus the mind one-pointedly, so Devadatta achieved this state of calm abiding and became able to manifest miracles, even though he did not have spiritual realization. He approached the king at that time and manifested his powers. As a consequence, the

king trusted him and became his follower. Then Devadatta manipulated the king into attacking the Buddha. All of this happened because at the outset the Arhat Kāśyapa did not discern properly. This kind of mistake can happen to arhats. Bodhisattvas may also make the mistake of not correctly discerning a particular situation. For example, some bodhisattvas were fooled by evil non-humans who approached them with the intention of creating obstacles. The evil non-humans requested them to offer the limbs of their body. It happened that some bodhisattvas who did not investigate the situation responded by offering their limbs. Buddhas would never make such a mistake. Even if millions of followers are present, buddhas always know in detail what each of them needs at all times and under all circumstances.

The realization of buddhas
(qualities 21–26)

(21) The seventh of the eighteen qualities is that a buddha's aspiration to keep the wheel of Dharma in motion never declines. In our era it was Buddha Śākyamuni who turned the wheel of Dharma. Since his lifetime has passed, it is clear that beings such as ourselves don't have the fortune to meet him, meaning we do not have the karma to meet the Buddha in person and receive teachings directly from him. It is not that the Buddha has disappeared from this world, is taking a rest somewhere, and stopped teaching. Whenever the karma to receive his Dharma

teachings ripens in sentient beings, he teaches. His aspiration to turn the wheel of Dharma never declines. In fact, the Buddha uninterruptedly turns the wheel of Dharma for sentient beings, making it available at all times. But from the perspective of sentient beings, the karma must be ripe to be able to receive these teachings.

(22) The eighth of the eighteen qualities is that a buddha's joyous effort to accomplish the benefit of sentient beings never declines. This kind of joyous effort is limitless. It is therefore very different from our own limited type of joyous effort, where we have to force ourselves in certain ways, really making an effort. A buddha's joyous effort is completely natural and benefits countless sentient beings without interruption. This joyous effort therefore does not imply any force from the perspective of a buddha.

(23) The ninth of the eighteen qualities is a buddha's never declining mindfulness. Generally, mindfulness literally means recollection. Yet here, it does not pertain to memory in an ordinary sense. It rather means that a buddha is capable in each and every moment of being mindful in detail of the variety, capacities, and karma of sentient beings. There is no interruption in this knowledge.

(24) The tenth of the eighteen qualities is that a buddha's meditative absorption never declines. This is similar to the eighteenth of the thirty-two powers explained above, where it is said that a buddha is in a state of meditative absorption at all times. The difference between these two is

that in the first context this refers to the behavior of a buddha, whereas here it refers to the mind of a buddha, which by nature is a state of meditative absorption. Unlike ordinary sentient beings, buddhas do not have to absorb themselves in meditation. Their very mind is meditative absorption.

(25) The eleventh of the eighteen qualities is insight, which in this context means omniscience. This insight cannot be compared to ordinary intelligence whereby knowledge about something is acquired based on discernment and investigation. A buddha's omniscience is not conditioned in that way. It is not a narrow, limited state of mind. It is insight in the sense that everything is known completely and simultaneously in one moment.

(26) This subdivision of six ends with the twelfth of the eighteen qualities. Because a buddha's insight is not stained by even the subtlest afflictive and cognitive obscuration, he or she possesses the quality called the vision of the wisdom of liberation.[7]

The activity of buddhas
(qualities 27–29)

(27) Buddhas physically manifest in different forms and perform different deeds in order to benefit sentient beings according to their needs. An example is the way the Buddha manifested in this world during our age. We must understand that he not only manifests in the human realm

55

as a human being, but also in many other forms according to what is appropriate to different realms and worlds. He may also manifest in inanimate forms, for example, as relics that are a source of blessing, or as self-arisen stūpas. He may manifest as beneficial substances such as medicinal plants that have no negative side effects, or as edible plants that meet the needs of sentient beings. Another example of the physical manifestation of a buddha is the pure land of Sukhāvatī, which is a manifestation of Buddha Amitābha.

(28) A buddha's verbal activities are to express Dharma teachings with the sixty qualities of his speech. For example, he teaches in a way that everybody who hears a buddha, hears the teaching in his or her own language.

(29) The mental activities of a buddha are that he is always full of perfect, continuous love and compassion for sentient beings that never declines.

These three aspects of buddha activity are interrelated, mutually causing each other.

The wisdom of buddhas
(qualities 30–32)

A buddha is all-knowing with respect to all objects of knowledge in each and every moment, whether this concerns the:

(30) past;
(31) future;

(32) or present. Whatever can be known is thus known by a buddha's wisdom. Nothing is ever mixed up or mistaken in any way. A buddha is never confused.

These are the thirty-two qualities of a buddha: the ten powers, the four types of fearlessness, and the eighteen qualities that are exclusive to a buddha. They are the qualities of the dharmakāya. In fact, these qualities are all inherent in the minds of all sentient beings. They are mind's nature here and now, the actual quality of our mind, our buddha nature. However, due to basic ignorance we are not aware of them, and they are not manifest. When basic ignorance is cleared away, these qualities will appear.

How can qualities be present but not manifest?

In order to help us understand how qualities can be present but not manifest, Buddhist schools of thought scrutinize mind and its workings. One of the models in which this is done is by distinguishing three aspects of mind: the imagined nature, the dependent nature, and the perfect nature. This topic is an important subject in Buddhist philosophy, particularly in the context of the Yogācāra[8] school of thought.

Let us first have a look at the "imagined nature." At present, our mind is in a state of ignorance because it is not aware of its own true nature. Due to this ignorance, our perceptions consist of deluded appearances. When we use the term "imagined nature," we refer to all these deluded appearances or perceptions. We might also say the entire world of appearance is created by the dualistic mind and does not exist in its own right. Phenomena appear to exist externally, but in fact they are mere deluded appearances, invented or imagined by an inner apprehender or grasper, that is, the capacity to perceive. The imagined nature comprises therefore both the "objects" that appear and the clinging mind that apprehends them. These are experienced as two different things, as subject and object. On this basis our entire samsaric experience of the world and our interaction with it takes place.

The "dependent nature" also designates an aspect of our mind in the state of ignorance, not the wisdom mind of a buddha. The dependent nature is polluted in the sense that it is the samsaric mind entirely under the influence of both poles of "subject" and "object"—a totality that it takes to be a real world. The samsaric mind is dependent on the subject-object projection that it mistakenly perceives. Being fully influenced by these perceptions it lacks freedom and is therefore called the dependent consciousness. In short, the dependent nature is our consciousness and its workings; it is our mind polluted by its delusion.

The "perfect nature" is the genuine true nature of the mind, the dharmakāya with the qualities specified above. It is the perfectly manifested presence of that which is naturally there. Therefore, it is called perfect wisdom. When this natural perfection is actualized, the true nature of mind is realized, and the mind is no longer under the sway of the imagined and dependent natures. Conversely, for as long as the true nature of mind is not realized, the imagined and dependent natures are operating.

We can also look at the question whether the imagined nature, the dependent nature, and the perfect nature actually exist or not.

Let us first examine the "imagined nature." Deluded appearances, which are the imagined nature, do not exist in their own right; they are fleeting and insubstantial. In fact, they are just confused manifestations that are created by the dualistic mind, resembling images in a dream that lack any true independent existence. Even though these appearances seem to exist in an outer world, they actually have no life on their own outside of the projecting mind. Because they have never really existed external to the mind, they also cannot be removed from it. It is not like removing, for example, impurities from the skin. The imagined nature thus does not exist and has never existed as such.

According to the Yogācāra philosophical school, the "dependent nature"—the projecting mind—exists in the sense that it is the mind itself. It is merely influenced by the imagined nature and in this way depends on it or we may say is polluted by it.

This also brings us to the "perfect nature," which according to the Yogācāra school exists as mind itself free from the dependent nature and the imagined nature. The Madhyamaka philosophical school holds a different opinion. According to this way of analyzing reality, mind itself does not truly exist either. Broadly speaking, in the Buddhist communities of India and Tibet, the Madhyamaka school is considered to be the highest Buddhist view, followed by the Yogācāra system. Yet, until you attain a high level of bodhisattva realization, you can never really say which view is lower and which is higher. All you can do is just follow the tradition and the assumption that the Madhyamaka view is higher. Until we ourselves are enlightened, we cannot say which view is the more supreme.

Both the Yogācāra and Madhyamaka schools agree that the imagined nature is empty, that it does not truly exist. They only differ on the question of whether or not mind itself exists. In fact, the Mādhyamikas usually, instead of using the template of the three natures, prefer to distinguish between a relative and an ultimate reality. And, although regarding the question of mind's actual existence the Yogācāra and Madhyamaka school are not in accordance, they are also not dramatically opposed to one another. Moreover, what is most important is that this disagreement does not cause any problems for a practitioner on the path. You may apply either view, because both are an adequate basis for meditation practice.

Regardless of what type of meditation you engage in, it is very helpful and important for your practice to have a clear understanding of these viewpoints because they concern mind, its nature, and its workings. When your view is accurate, the meditation will unfold in the right way without mistakes and problems. This is because Buddhist meditation is about working with the mind. So if you do not have a good understanding of mind's processes and nature, you will tend to make mistakes in practice. Therefore, a good understanding of the mind is needed in order to become a good meditator.

The special qualities of the form kāyas

The different qualities of the dharmakāya describe the state of wisdom that is buddhahood itself. They are the qualities of the awakened state. Inseparable from the qualities of the dharmakāya is the way in which it is of benefit to sentient beings, its manifestations. These manifestations and their qualities are called the form kāyas. The form kāya comprises both the sambhogakāya and the nirmāṇakāya. These two form kāyas are not like Kṛṣṇa or any other god that is believed to abide somewhere in another dimension. The dharmakāya and the two form kāyas are the nature of mind itself, the mental continuum of each and every sentient being.

The sambhogakāya is perceptible to bodhisattvas who abide on the bhūmis, which means to beings who have transcended the samsaric mind but are not yet fully enlightened. As the bodhisattvas have a very pure mind with a great accumulation of merit and wisdom, they are able to enjoy the pure buddha worlds and the manifestations of buddhahood as the sambhogakāya. Ordinary impure beings can only perceive the nirmāṇakāya, the emanation body. One should not look at these two form kāyas in terms of higher and lower, however. From the perspective of the two kāyas there is no such distinction. It is only a matter of what sentient beings are able to perceive based on their state of mind, based on their merit and wisdom.

Both the dharmakāya and the form kāyas abide in our mind, and the basic cause for realizing the form kāyas is the dharmakāya itself. It might be compared with the sun, which is the basic cause for sunlight to manifest. What makes the form kāyas manifest is an accumulation of merit gathered on the bodhisattva's path during a period of the three so- called immeasurable eons. By virtue of this merit, when the bodhisattva attains ultimate enlightenment—actualizes the dharmakāya—the form kāyas spontaneously manifest for the benefit of all sentient beings. This process begins the first time bodhicitta is generated, both in its aspiration and application aspects. From then on it continues with the virtue that goes along with benefiting sentient beings. Beginner bodhisattvas are able to generate small amounts of virtue. This small amount of merit grows and multiplies, as each virtuous act is a cause for more substantial actions, like a chain reaction. In this way the merit becomes larger and larger until the bodhisattva can engage in a limitless amount of virtuous activities. Accordingly, the bodhisattva progresses through the paths of accumulation and preparation, where the capacity to perform virtuous actions is already amazingly great. Eventually, he or she achieves the path of vision, and with it the first bodhisattva bhūmi. With the progress through the bhūmis the scale on which virtue is accomplished multiplies until it is immeasurable. When the ten bhūmis are finally completed, buddhahood is attained. With this full realization of the dharmakāya, the merit that was generated throughout this whole process manifests as the form kāyas for the uninterrupted benefit of others.

It is through the power of bodhicitta that this chain reaction of virtue comes about. One virtuous deed works as the cause for the next, and in this way merit multiplies and becomes immeasurable. Without bodhicitta this isn't possible. Regardless of how great it may be, virtue generated without bodhicitta will merely ripen as positive results, thereby exhausting itself. If great bodhicitta is generated, however, even if a virtuous deed seems to be insignificant, it will act as a cause for further and further virtue and will thus ever increase. It will never come to an end, as it is not bound to one's personal welfare but dedicated to the benefit of all sentient beings. For this reason bodhicitta is understood to be at the root of all qualities, and in particular the root of the attainment of buddhahood.

In short, the dharmakāya is mainly realized through the power of wisdom, and the two form kāyas manifest mainly through the power of merit. At the same time, the dharmakāya and the form kāyas are the very nature of our own mind here and now. Still, unless methods are applied to accomplish them—the accumulation of merit and wisdom— the dharmakāya and the form kāyas remain hidden.

How exactly is this manifestation of the form kāyas to be understood? What kind of bodies manifest? In order to understand that, we must first take a look at our present deluded samsaric state. At present we don't perceive our dharmakāya, and this leads to a deluded experience that is the exact opposite of the true nature of mind and its qualities. We simply perceive our samsaric mind and are deluded. Consequently, the deluded samsaric mind leads to a physical appearance that is similarly impure or deluded. The samsaric mind clings to a self where there is no self, which in turn gives rise to afflictions. These afflictions in turn motivate actions that then propel us into rebirths in a deluded world with a physical body. The specific type of world and body depend on the karma accumulated. As human beings, our particular body and the corresponding world we inhabit are due to each person's individual karma. The same holds true for other states. For example, in the animal realm an elephant has its own particular body. A fish living in the water has its particular body, and so does a bird flying in the sky. All of this is caused by the previous karmic actions of the individual beings. In this way, all of these beings have bodies that are nothing but appearances from the samsaric mind.

When all confusion is cleared away from the mind, these deluded manifestations no longer appear. Instead, the mind that has been realized as the dharmakāya manifests in pure appearances and bodies, which are the two form kāyas.

As these form kāyas and their true qualities have nothing to do with the way a samsaric mind in the human realm works, they are actually inconceivable to the mind of an ordinary person. They simply do not fit into our human range of perception. It is purely for the sake of our becoming somehow able to relate to them that these bodies and their qualities are described using language and concepts that we can understand and relate to. Therefore, the statement, "when the mind is actualized as the state of dharmakāya, the corresponding qualities manifest as the form kāyas" tries to give us a certain idea, taking our present state as an example to illustrate the process of manifestation. Intellectually, we can understand that, just as based on a deluded mind, the impure body and its environment manifests, based on a pure mind, the pure dharmakāya and the form kāyas manifest. It is important to be aware that this is an intellectual understanding only, and does not mean we truly know the form kāyas. Our way of relating to things through our sense faculties and neurotic states of consciousness are far too limited for that. We should therefore not be fixated on our ideas regarding the nature of the form kāyas, imagining that they are like this or like that. Our ideas about them cannot be accurate. We might think that the sambhogakāyas are more or less like our own bodies, only far more beautiful, majestic, and powerful, etc. But they don't resemble our bodies at all. We should not think, for example, that the sambhogakāya and nirmāṇakāya bodies go to a café the same way we go to a café.

The most important thing to understand here is that once the impurities of the mind are cleared away, the dharmakāya and the form kāyas are attained. In this sense, the cause of buddhahood and manifestations for the benefit of others are the two accumulations of merit and wisdom. And the result is the realization of the dharmakāya, the sambhogakāya, and the nirmāṇakāya.

Purification of obscurations

The various obscurations that affect the mind are purified progressively. The first obscurations that need to be purified are the afflictions: desire, anger, ignorance, envy, pride, jealousy, etc. This is the process we go through on the paths of accumulation and preparation. When these afflictive obscurations are done away with, we attain the path of vision

and thus the first bodhisattva bhūmi. At this point
the obvious obscurations associated with afflictions
are completely purified. But there still remain
cognitive obscurations with respect to objects of
knowledge. These obstructions consist of grasping
at the characteristics of deluded appearances that
are projected by the mind. As we progress from
the first through to the seventh bhūmi, we are for
the most part progressively purifying ourselves of
these cognitive obscurations. But even at the stage
of the seventh bhūmi very subtle obscurations still
limit the mind. These obscure our samādhi and are
called the obscurations of meditative absorption.
They prevent the bodhisattva from experiencing
ultimate and perfect meditative absorption. At this
stage of development, even though you are at a high
bodhisattva level, you will not yet have achieved
the wisdom of buddhahood. On the eighth, ninth
and tenth bhūmis these obscurations are purified as
well. Having gone through this process, you finally
realized the ultimate wisdom of buddhahood.

To put these achievements in perspective, you
should understand that with the attainment of the
first bhūmi, the sufferings and problems of cyclic
existence have been overcome. That is why this state
of realization must not be underestimated. As we
strive for the attainment of buddhahood, we might
imagine that the first bodhisattva bhūmi is not such
an extraordinary achievement. However, the first
bhūmi is an amazing realization and is not easily
attained. Once you have attained the first bhūmi,
you are naturally heading for all the subsequent
bodhisattva levels one after the other until the
realization of buddhahood. Those who attain the

first bodhisattva bhūmi are therefore very advanced practitioners and certainly not people who are entangled in the problems of ordinary life.

The all-accomplishing wisdom

Buddhahood manifests for the benefit of sentient beings and therefore does not have deluded appearances. Rather, it appears as the all-accomplishing wisdom wherein all actions are spontaneously fulfilled. For this reason it is also referred to as buddha activities. These activities are the appearance of the two form kāyas.

Let's take another look at the process of an ordinary being's manifestation. Due to their karma, sentient beings are reborn in their respective bodies and corresponding environments. They experience form, sound, smell, taste, touch, and mental objects, on the basis of which they react by grasping at what seems pleasant or beneficial to themselves and their close ones, and rejecting what seems unpleasant. In constantly making these distinctions, they are lost in their delusion, being neither mindful nor at peace. It is a very coarse state wherein we grasp at the mind as the inner subject (our self), and at appearances—the perceived world—as external objects. We then perceive everything on the basis of this dualistic distinction. In this way the subject-object relationship based on grasping, rejection, and indifference takes place. This is how the world of ordinary beings functions, with all its problems and difficulties.

The form kāyas, on the other hand, manifest by virtue of the dharmakāya. They are the all-accomplishing wisdom and are free of all such dualistic clinging. Perception experienced as wisdom free of dualistic clinging is no longer under the sway of ordinary form, sound, smell, taste, touch, and thought. Grasping and aversion, adopting and rejecting, do not take place. For example, the enlightened yogi Milarepa was not limited by dualistic clinging or ordinary perception. He once manifested himself inside a small yak horn. He did so without performing the miracle of shrinking his body or of enlarging the horn. Still he could place his body into the yak horn. How is this possible? Categories like "small" and "big" are nothing but the result of dualistic clinging. It is because we cling to the concepts of "small" and "big" that we are not capable of placing our bodies into a small yak horn. Enlightened beings, who have freed themselves from the trap of dualistic concepts and their limitations, are able to do anything because they are no longer influenced by clinging.

In our case, we perceive an impure world due to dualistic clinging. Based on the six sense fields, impure form, sound, smell, taste, touch, and mental objects are experienced. An enlightened individual, on the other hand, experiences the pure world of the saṃbhogakāya with all its perfect qualities, and accomplishes the benefit of sentient beings. An enlightened being can do this by virtue of wisdom free of dualistic notions. This is how Buddha Amitābha manifests the pure world Sukhāvatī, supporting sentient beings to take rebirth in his pure world and thereby enabling them to proceed to the enlightened state of a buddha. The capacity to do all this is the all-accomplishing wisdom, and is the activity or wisdom of the two form kāyas.

Sentient beings are limitless in number, and accordingly the all-accomplishing wisdom performs limitless actions in order to benefit them. As pointed out above, the basis of the all-accomplishing wisdom is complete freedom from dualistic notions. By virtue of this power, pure kāyas and pure worlds manifest in all kinds of ways. This activity is in support of countless sentient beings in ways that are beneficial to them, provided they have the karma to be accessible to it. This condition must be there. Whenever the openness to enlightened activity is present, the supportive activity manifests immediately. Another aspect of this activity is to mature those beings who are not yet ripe. The following is an example. The saṃbhogakāya and the pure worlds of the saṃbhogakāya can only be perceived by realized bodhisattvas. Before these realized bodhisattvas attained this spiritual achievement, they were ordinary sentient beings who found the path and methods to develop and cultivate bodhicitta. That they were able to find the path and methods is due to buddha activity. By applying the methods and paths, these individuals developed into realized bodhisattvas on the bhūmis, enabling them to encounter the saṃbhogakāya and experience the pure worlds.

We can also look at this from another perspective. As we already know, the source of all methods and paths is bodhicitta. Once we realize mind's true nature, mind starts manifesting for the benefit of others because of the very presence of bodhicitta, because this has been our intention since our first steps on the bodhisattva path. Again, this happens because of buddha activity. In a way, bodhicitta resembles a mother, and buddhahood her child.

We may also say that the dharmakāya is like the sun in the sky. The sun emits rays of light that correspond to the form kāyas. The effect is that the warmth of these rays of light matures all kinds of seeds that are in the earth, and the process of this ripening is referred to as the all- accomplishing wisdom.

The wisdom that knows the variety of appearances

The wisdom and associated activities of buddhahood are limitless. They correspond to the equally limitless varieties of confusion, deluded appearances, and perceptions of sentient beings. The wisdom and activities of buddhahood support sentient beings in purifying themselves of impurities, and in the ways it benefits others, the state of buddhahood can be said to be like the sky. All kinds of clouds may appear in the sky. There are white clouds or black clouds, and the wind blows them around so that all kinds of cloud formations occur. The nature of the sky itself, however, never changes. It is never tainted by all these formations or appearances. Likewise, a buddha's state of wisdom sees and relates to all kinds of ordinary and pure beings, but is never affected by their karma or their perceptions. The capacity to see exactly what is necessary in each particular case is called the wisdom that sees everything in all its variety, and this wisdom's associated activities reach sentient beings everywhere.

The wisdom of equality

Ordinary sentient beings identify with their ground consciousness. They cling to it as a self and are therefore limited by their dualistic clinging. As we have seen above, this clinging gives rise to the experience of a dualistic realm based on the concept of self and other. In buddhahood this clinging to duality is completely purified, and this state of being purified of all clinging to duality is called the wisdom of equality. The activity of the wisdom of equality is that a buddha never strays from the total peace of the dharmakāya, while at the same time uninterruptedly accomplishing the benefit of sentient beings. This basically happens once the stain of clinging to the ground consciousness as a self and all the associated dualistic clinging are eliminated. When these defilements have dissipated, dualistic clinging within the cycle of existence does not reoccur.

The difference between an arhat and a buddha

Buddhas abide in the sphere of the dharmakāya. This state is not the same as the meditative absorption achieved by an arhat, either through the Śrāvaka- or the Pratyekabuddhayāna. Arhats do not accomplish the benefit of sentient beings through the two form kāyas, and they have not arrived at the ultimate fruition of the path. They have purified their minds of all afflictions and are therefore free of the impurity of karma. They have transcended karmic causes and effects. But as they have not fully perfected their meditative absorption, they continue to abide in one particular type of it. Contrary to this, in the wisdom of a buddha all meditative absorptions are spontaneously perfected. Never wavering from a state of meditative absorption, while being in a state of total peace, buddhas naturally benefit sentient beings.

The form kāyas do not resemble an ordinary body

The two form kāyas should not be understood to be like our own bodies or the other constituents of the five skandhas, that is, form, sensations, distinctions, compositional factors, and consciousness. The body as part of the five skandhas is a result of afflictions and karma. It is therefore impure, and suffering goes along with it. The two form kāyas, on the other hand, are spontaneous expressions of wisdom. They are not the result of contaminated afflictions and actions. Therefore, the form kāyas do not resemble our physical bodies.

Ignorance and illusory appearances do not reoccur

Mind's true nature is the buddha nature, which at present is obscured by ignorance. You may wonder if there is a danger that ignorance can return even after the mind is purified from all impurities and buddhahood is attained. This will not happen. Buddhahood is definitive. This is because buddhahood is realized by virtue of the personally experienced wisdom of self-awareness. Mind in this state is no longer anything but wisdom, and it therefore cannot possibly return to a state of ignorance. Buddhahood will never deteriorate.

Likewise, you may also wonder if the illusory appearances of cyclic existence may manifest again. The answer is the same; they do not reoccur. This is because of the way illusory appearances manifest in the perception of ordinary beings. When an ordinary sentient being clings to the ground consciousness as a self, the various afflictions, karma, and so on arise. This entire process does not reoccur in buddhahood for the very reason that the mind is personally experienced as wisdom. This wisdom realizes that afflictions and illusory appearances do not have a nature of their own; they do not really exist. Thus, to a mind that is fully aware of this, afflictions and illusory appearances cannot become real existents. They are exclusively the experience of a mind that is deluded. Therefore, once the mind is without delusion in a state of realized wisdom, these deluded appearances do not reoccur. It resembles the situation where you have awoken from a dream, and in your waking state the dream is simply gone.

Buddha nature resembles gold ore

Buddha wisdom with all its qualities is the essence of our mind stream and can be compared to gold ore. When gold is in its unrefined form, it is mixed with stones and earth. However, when we clear away the stones and the earth, we are able to extract the gold, enabling all of its different qualities to manifest. If, on the other hand, we don't make any effort to purify the gold in this way, when we just look at the gold ore, it is simply black earth or stone. At the same time, if there were no gold within the stone, no matter how much effort we put into purifying it, we would not succeed in finding gold. If there is no gold to begin with, there is no possibility of making it appear. However, gold ore contains gold; it is simply encased in all kinds of impurities. The same holds true for the mind: it is buddha nature but encased in obscurations. If we purify our mind, when these impurities are cleared away, we will discover mind's inherent wisdom.

Purification: its basis, object, method, and result

The basis of purification

The basis of purification is our present mind, which is obscured by the veil of ignorance, and therefore projects deluded appearances. This is the context in which we have to carry out the purification.

The object of purification

What must be cleared away are all the obscurations: first the coarse or obvious ones, and later the subtle ones. The coarse obscurations are the afflictions, the karmic seeds, and the karmic results. The subtle obscurations are cognitive obscurations regarding objects of knowledge, and the very subtle obscurations are those regarding meditative absorption.

Afflictions consist of all the negative states of mind, both intense and subtle, including ignorance and doubts. The obscuration of karmic seeds consists of all the suffering- producing tendencies that are stored in the mind stream as a consequence of our constant actions. Karmic results come about due to these tendencies. These karmic results are the obscuration of the ripened situations sentient beings find themselves in, the places where they are reborn and so on. It is important to be aware of the fact that due to their karma, innumerable sentient beings do not have the great good fortune to be reborn as human beings. They may be reborn as animals, for instance. In this case, they don't have the possibility to follow a spiritual path, to differentiate between good and bad, and are not able to find a path that leads to freedom from suffering. Another example is the karmic result of being reborn in the hell realms.

These are examples of the obscurations that are karmic results. The obscurations of karmic seeds and of karmic results are both triggered by the obscurations of the afflictions. Among these, the most dangerous obscurations are karmic results.

In order to protect ourselves from these we must purify the obscurations of karmic seeds. And to be able to avoid the new accumulation of karmic seeds, we must purify ourselves of the obscurations of the afflictions. These three—afflictions, karmic seeds, and karmic results—are thus interrelated. As long as they govern the mind, there is no chance to free ourselves from cyclic existence, because we continuously recreate the same process producing the illusion of cyclic existence. Therefore, to begin with we must overcome these three types of obscurations. Once we have overcome them, it will be easy to overcome the subtle cognitive obscurations and the very subtle ones regarding meditative absorption, which prevent us from entering a perfect state of samādhi.

The method of purification

The Kagyu tradition emphasizes in this regard the method of Mahāmudrā and does so in two ways. On the one hand, there is the method of purification in terms of the tantric Six Yogas of Nāropa (1016–1100). This approach is called the path of methods. On the other hand, there is the method of purification based on particular key instructions according to Maitrīpa (986–1063), the teachings of Mental Non-engagement (Sanskrit: *amanasikāra*). Here, four yogas with all in all twelve progressive steps toward the realization of Mahāmudrā are distinguished.

This approach is called the path of liberation.[9] Both of these transmissions were brought to Tibet by Marpa, the translator. Either of these approaches is suitable, and will enable practitioners to completely overcome the obscurations that are preventing them from realizing the true nature of mind: buddha nature. Once all the impurities are cleared away, all of the different qualities of wisdom that have been described in this text will appear.

The result of purification

Buddha wisdom is the result of purification.

Concluding advice

This concludes my explanation based on *Revealing Buddha Nature,* which was composed by Karmapa Rangjung Dorje. Like his treatise *Distinguishing Between Consciousness and Wisdom,* this text is of great importance for Dharma practitioners and for an understanding of Buddhist philosophy.

When practicing the Dharma, we should apply the flawless methods progressively from the very beginning. These methods will purify our mind stream of impurities and thus allow for our liberation from cyclic existence and attainment of awakening. This level is attained by clearing ignorance from our mind so that mind's true nature can reveal itself.

Regarding the methods that can be used to clear the impurities from our mind, we might be tempted to rely on our own opinions about what methods will bring good results and help us attain enlightenment. We may put our faith in different kinds of philosophy and psychology, and so on. However, we should recognize that such methods are limited and consequently that if we rely on them in order to reach enlightenment, we are similar to a blind person wandering around in the many streets of a big town. There is no certainty about this person's destination. If instead we apply perfect and well-tested methods, it is as if that same blind person's eyesight is restored. Now he or she can arrive at the desired destination without fail. We should therefore rely on the right methods from the very beginning. Rely on a spiritual friend, and then practice uninterruptedly until you reach the state of awakening.

Revealing Buddha Nature

A treatise by the
3rd Karmapa, Rangjung Dorje

Paying homage[10]

I pay homage to all the buddhas and bodhisattvas.

Short explanation based on scriptures
From the Abhidharma Sūtra:
It is said: "Though beginningless, it has an end.
The pure phenomenon that by nature is always
[the same] is not beheld because it is obscured by
beginningless veils. It is, for example, just like a
hidden golden statue."[11]
"The [buddha] element has been the basis for all
phenomena since beginningless time. Because it
exists, [there are] all beings, and nirvāṇa is also
attained."

From the Hevajra Tantra:
"Sentient beings are indeed buddhas, yet, they are obscured by adventitious stains. Once these are removed, they are buddhas."[12] [This is a] quote from a tantra.

Detailed meaning according to the Abhidharma Sūtra
On being beginningless:
In this context, "beginningless" means that prior to it there is nothing.
Time is this very moment.
How could it come from somewhere else?

The meaning of the buddha element:[13]
The [buddha] element is without a creator, yet because it has its own characteristics it is labeled that way.

The phenomena that are based on it:
The phenomena are saṃsāra and nirvāṇa, explained as twofold appearance.
That is called "ground of tendencies of ignorance."
The movement of the formations of correct and incorrect conceptualizations is the producing cause.
The causal condition is explained as the "ground."

The buddha element as a basis:
The basis is buddha nature.
Incorrect conceptualizations are based solely on the purity of the mind.

How buddha nature exists at present:
This purity exists precisely at this moment.
Although it exists,

due to ignorant conceptualization
it is not beheld, and there is saṃsāra.

The meaning of "end":
When they are removed, it is nirvāṇa,
which conventionally is called the "end."

An explanation of correct and incorrect conceptualization
How saṃsāra is based on incorrect conceptualization:
Beginning and end depend purely on
conceptualization. Formations, which are similar to
the wind, give rise to actions and afflictions.
Through these, the manifestations of all phenomena
of dualistic appearances [come about]:
the skandhas, dhātus, and āyatanas.[14]

The root of delusion: adopting and rejecting:
The one who adopts and rejects is deluded.
By rejecting [mind's] own appearances,
where should they cease?
By adopting [mind's] own appearances, what is
achieved? Is this dualistic clinging not deceptive?

The meaning of thoughts as antidotes:
Knowledge of this is indeed taught as a remedy.
Thoughts about non-duality are not reality, however,
as that which is free of concepts is conceptualized.
Having understood that forms, and so on,
are empty by splitting them into parts,
are you not in a state of delusion?
Nevertheless, this was taught in order to bring
clinging to reality to an end.

Explaining the essence of buddha nature itself:
All is neither real nor delusive.
Wise ones maintain it resembles [the reflection of the] moon in water.
This natural awareness is precisely what is called dharmadhātu, the nature of the Victors.
It is not turned good by the noble ones; it is not turned bad by sentient beings. Although it is described through many terms, its meaning is not understood through description.

Explaining the qualities
Short explanation:
[That] its unimpeded display comprises sixty-four [buddha-]qualities is a rough [description]; each of these is said to comprise tens of millions [of qualities].

Detailed explanation:
The thirty-two qualities of the dharmakāya,
beginning with the ten powers
[1] Knowledge of what is a basis and what is not a basis.
[2] Knowledge of karmic actions and [their] fruits,
[3] of nature, [4] of capacities,
[5] of intentions, [6] of all existing paths,
[7] and of meditative absorptions.
[8] The divine eye,
[9] recollecting existences, and [10] peace.
These are the ten powers.[15]

The four types of fearlessness
Based on these are the four types of fearlessness:
[11] indisputability when displaying awakening with respect to all phenomena,

when [12] teaching the obstacles,
and when [13] teaching the path and [14] cessation.[16]

The eighteen unique qualities
Based on this cause, the eighteen [qualities] are:
[15] non-delusion; [16] no chatter;
[17] unhindered awareness; [18] constant
meditative absorption;
[19] free of conceptual distinctions;
[20] free of lack of discernment;
[21] unimpaired striving, [22] joyous effort,
[23] recollection,
[24] meditative absorption, [25] insight
[26] and vision of the wisdom of liberation;
[27–29] wisdom precedes actions;
[30–32] being unobscured with regard to time.[17]
Being endowed with these thirty-two [qualities] is
the dharmakāya.

How it is that they do not appear,
even though they are present now:
At present, the opposite of these is taking place.
By not determining that which is or the way it
is, the non-existent is seen to exist, creating the
imagined [nature].
The conceptualizations produced thereby
are the dependent [nature].
Unaware of the perfect [nature]
we are entangled in our own doings.
Alas, when these qualities of the dharmakāya
are realized to be real,
this is knowledge of reality.
[Even] the present few capacities are reality.
By casting away this knowledge, we produce the
unreal and are taken in by the agitation of pursuing it.

How this is realized, including scriptural support:
By virtue of now knowing what is, as it is,
you attain power in it.
"From here, there is nothing to be removed,
and not the slightest thing to be added.
Reality is to be seen as it is.
By seeing reality, liberation [is achieved]."[18]
"The [buddha] element is empty of the
adventitious, which is characterized as separable.
But it is not empty of the unsurpassable qualities,
that are characterized as inseparable."[19]

The qualities of the form kāyas
The essence of the qualities:
Therein, the nature of the two form kāyas,
consists of the thirty-two signs and marks.

Justification that they dwell in the body:
The qualities obtained are one's own body.
This body is not produced by a Self, Fate, Īśvara,
Brahmā, real external particles, or something hidden.
When this impure manifestation of subject and
object of the five [sense] gates has been purified,
then the term "attainment" is applied.

The manner of purity and impurity:
Therefore, when the energy channels, currents,
and potencies[20] are purified, they are the pure form
kāyas. Unpurified they are the impure form kāyas.

Explanation by means of an example
The example:
For example, an untreated blue beryl's qualities
are not apparent.

Only after it is cleansed, purified with cloth and
alkaline solution, cleaned with acid and a woolen
cloth and polished with clear water and finest Kāśī
fabric, does it become pure, the jewel that is the
source for all needs.

Associating the example with the meaning:
It is the same with the blue beryl of mind:
to remove the three veils—those of afflictions,
those with respect to objects of knowledge and
those of meditative absorption—we must fully
purify ourselves on the paths of accumulation and
preparation, the seven impure [bodhisattva] levels
and the three pure ones.

How the two obscurations are overcome, in order:
When correct concepts meet the incorrect ones,
we are freed from all concepts—just like two
wooden sticks being burned equally. [This is]
freedom from the four types of clinging: at what is
to be given up, the remedies, concepts regarding
reality, and fruition.

*How purity is attained even though buddha nature is unchanging,
including scriptural support:*
At that point, in those who are endowed with the
space[-like] kāya,
the flower of the marks will blossom.
"According to the stages of impure, impure and
pure, and utterly pure, the three states of sentient
beings, bodhisattvas and tathāgatas
are described."[21]
However, buddhahood is nothing newly arisen.
"As it was before, so it is later.

Such is the unchanging buddha nature."[22]
Becoming free from stains,
this is what is called change.

Ascertainment through answers to objections
Summary of how the qualities neither occur without causes,
nor from outer causes:
Those who follow wrong views think that buddha
qualities are either without cause or are produced
by external causes and conditions
that are not in ourselves.
How does this differ from the eternalism
and nihilism of non-Buddhists?

Certainty with regard to the pure and impure mind:
The appearance of formations that arise and cease
momentarily is similar to the impure formations.
If it were not like that, the activity of the form
kāyas would be interrupted. However, this is not
expressed with the term "formations" but rather
with "distinguishing wisdom."

The essence of the all-accomplishing wisdom:
How subject and object of the five gates appear
That which has the nature of the great elements,
and so on, and is associated with clinging,
shows its powerful essence.
Regarding appearances, there is not the slightest
difference between delusion and non-delusion.

The difference between sentient beings and buddhas:
The difference is whether or not there is
clinging to duality. If it were not like that, how
could a buddha's activity reach [sentient beings]?

The activity of the all-accomplishing wisdom,
the purpose of the analogy:
The use of analogies like the wish-fulfilling jewel,
illustrate that the powers display [themselves] free
from concepts...

The mistake of maintaining that buddha activity only appears
in the mind stream of others:
...but not that they merely [manifest]
in the mind stream of others.
If that were the case, the mind streams of others
would become wisdom.
If this is maintained, wisdom is delusion.

The certainty that appearances are not necessarily delusion,
along with a counterexample:
If it is alleged that [wisdom] clings to its own
appearances, a mirror would also have concepts of
clinging to what appears in it.

The wisdom of variety is not deluded— explaining the exam-
ple and its meaning:
The entire variety of sentient beings' delusion
appears as objects of wisdom.
However, wisdom is not contaminated by delusion;
just as the arising and cessation of great elements
appears in space, yet space is not contaminated and
does arise and cease.[23]

The meaning of [buddha nature] being connected with en-
lightened activity:
In the same way, the Victor's wisdom reaches
sentient beings but is without contamination.
In this case, the term "delusion" is not used, rather
it is called "all-accomplishing [wisdom]."

The meaning of the wisdom of equality:
Mind that abides purified of the three obscurations
is equality, which is also peace.
Being endowed with loving kindness and
great compassion, it appears [to beings] as
saṃbhoga[kāya] and in other [forms].
This is said in order to refute the [view] of some
that the attainment of buddhahood corresponds
with [an arhat of] the hīnayāna.

*Explanation of how the three kāyas are permanent, and The
meaning of the three kinds of permanence:*
Wisdom is permanent in three ways:
being permanent by nature is the dharmakāya;
being permanent in terms of continuity is the
saṃbhogakāya; and in being uninterrupted
is the nirmāṇakāya.[24]

The meaning of the three kinds of impermanence:
In this context, there are three phenomena that are
impermanent: intellectually produced emptiness is
not permanent; the movements of the conceptual
mind are not permanent; and the six conditioned
collections are not permanent.

Explaining these, respectively, as wisdom and stains:
Yet, in these there are three permanences. Whereas
the three impermanences are stains, the three kinds
of permanences are wisdom itself.

Overcoming uncertainty
How it is not being equivalent to the self of non-Buddhists:
[Buddha nature] is not equivalent to the self of
non-Buddhists which is imputed by the mind, because it is not imputed.

How it is unlike the peace of śrāvakas and pratyekabuddhas:
It is not equivalent to the peace of śrāvakas and
pratyekabuddhas, because it displays all qualities of
the form kāyas.

How it is unlike sentient beings:
These [form kāyas] are not equivalent to the bodies
of sentient beings, because they are not produced
by the contaminated conditions
[of karma and kleśas].

The meaning of not regressing:
[Buddhas] will never regress, because what is, is
manifest just as it is.

The meaning of defilements never reoccurring:
Defilements will never arise again, because it is
freedom from all concepts of difference.

Summary:
Therefore, mind itself is buddhahood.
Although this exists at present, we are unaware of it.

*Establishing certainty by explaining the actual essence
through scriptures*
From the Ornament of Mahāyāna Sūtras:
As soon as this is realized, at that time, "like the
fading of heat from iron and of blurred vision from
the eyes is [the fading of delusions] in a buddha's
mind and wisdom. It cannot be declared either
existent or nonexistent."[25]

From the Twenty Verses of the Mahāyāna by Nāgārjuna:
"Since ultimately there is no arising,

in reality there is also no liberation.
Buddhahood resembles space and sentient beings
have the same characteristics. As here [saṃsāra]
and there [nirvāṇa] are not arisen,
by nature nirvāṇa also does not exist.
Therefore, the conditioned is evidently empty;
[this] is the sphere of all-knowing wisdom."[26]

From the Ultimate Continuum of the Mahāyāna:
"Because it is subtle, it is not an object of learning.
Because it is ultimate, it is not one of reflecting.
Because it is the profound nature of reality, it is not
an object of worldly meditations, and so on."[27]

Summary of the meaning taught in the sūtras and tantras:
This is the sphere of the wisdom of self-awareness;
by virtue of self-arisen confidence,
the ultimate is brought forth.
Alas, because they do not realize this mode of
being, childlike beings wander around
in the ocean of saṃsāra.

Conclusion
How the text was composed:
By the power of the Great Sage [Śākyamuni],
Mañjughoṣa, Maitreya and Avalokiteśvara, [I],
Rangjung Dorje, composed this text.

Wishing prayer:
May all beings understand the buddha nature
perfectly and unmistakenly.
This completes the ascertainment of buddha nature,
the essence of the vajrayāna.

Śubhaṃ

Endnotes

1 In "A Clear Mirror of Pointing-Out Instructions Regarding One's Mind," *Rang sems ngo sprod gsal ba'i me long,* 195/6–196/2 and 194/3-6.

2 For example, the Buddha declared in the *Anamatagga Saṃyutta* of the Pāli canon (S II 179), that the first beginning of existence is something inconceivable, and that such notions and speculations of a beginning may lead to mental derangement.

3 Regarding the term "bodhicitta," please refer to the introduction.

4 In other contexts, for example in teachings that Shamar Rinpoche gave in his Bodhi Path center in Germany in 2004, he referred to this type of bodhicitta as the so-called "shepherd-like bodhicitta." It is an example of a bodhisattva's attitude

that first and foremost is concerned with other sentient beings' well-being, through the power of which, the bodhisattva naturally, yet slowly, proceeds toward his or her own attainment of buddhahood. In classical Mahāyāna literature, this terminology, i.e., shepherd-like bodhicitta," is frequently provided.

5 In 2004, Shamar Rinpoche referred to this attitude as the "king- like bodhicitta." It is an example of a bodhisattva's attitude that, grounded in the altruistic motivation to benefit others, enables a bodhisattva to strive for his or her own attainment of buddhahood first in order to help others on this basis, just like a king who with his royal powers, can help others. Again, in classical Mahāyāna literature, this terminology is frequently provided.

6 As long as an arhat is still alive, he or she still lives with what "remains" from previous karma and afflictions, that is, the body, even though he or she has freed the mind from veils. Once the arhat dies, this "remainder" ceases as well. Therefore, this state of cessation is referred to as "without remainder." It is a purely mental state where all samsaric ties have ceased, and thus no rebirth takes place.

7 The term "vision of the wisdom of liberation" emphasizes that, not just the obscurations that fetter an individual to cyclic existence, but also those that prevent the attainment of perfect buddhahood, are relinquished. This is what is meant by the remark that even the subtlest afflictive and cognitive obscurations are overcome.

8 The two main philosophical schools of Mahāyā-na Buddhism are called Yogācāra or Cittamātra (Mind-only) and Madhyamaka (Middle Way).

9 In his book *Boundless Wisdom: A Mahamudra Practice Manual,* Shamar Rinpoche gives detailed instructions on this approach.

10 The text that appears in italics and a smaller font is based on Kongtrul Lodrö Thaye's commentary, *De bzhin gshegs pa'i snying po bstan pa'i bstan bcos kyi rnam 'grel rang byung dgongs gsal.* For an English translation of it, see Brunnhölzl, *Luminous Heart,* Snow Lion Publications 2009.

11 This verse is quoted frequently in various treatises, yet the text as such is not extant.

12 Hevajratantra, part 2, IV.69.

13 The terms "element" and "buddha element" are translations of the Tibetan term *khams,* which literally means "element" or "basic constituent," and refers to the potency of qualities. It is a synonym here for buddha nature.

14 The five skandhas or aggregates are: form, sensation, distinction, compositional factors, and consciousness. The eighteen dhātus or elements are: the six sense organs, the six types of sense consciousness, and the six sense objects. The twelve āyatanas or sense fields are: the six sense organs with their respective consciousness, and the six sense objects.

15 The description of the ten powers resembles and summarizes *Uttaratantraśāstra* III.5–6.

16 The description of the four fearlessnesses is similar to *Uttaratantraśāstra* III.8.

17 The description of the eighteen unique qualities resembles and summarizes *Uttaratantraśāstra* III.11–13.

18 Quote from *Uttaratantraśāstra* I.154. The quote also appears in a number of other śāstras.

19 Quote from *Uttaratantraśāstra* I.155. 20 That is, nāḍīs, prāṇa and bindu.

21 Quote from *Uttaratantraśāstra* I.47. 22 Quote from *Uttaratantraśāstra* I.51cd.

23 A summary of *Uttaratantraś*āstra I.53–57 and 62. 24 Quote from the *Mahāyānasūtrālaṃkāra* IX.66cd. 25 Quote from *Mahāyānasūtrālaṃkāra* IX.25.

26 Quote from *Mahāyānaviṃśikā*, V.2–3.

27 Quote from *Uttaratantraśāstra* II.32.

About the Author

Shamar Rinpoche, Mipham Chökyi Lodrö (1952–2014), was the 14th Shamarpa. The Shamarpa or "Red Hat Lama of Tibet" is Tibetan Buddhism's second oldest reincarnate lineage after the Karmapa's lineage. Born in Derge, Tibet, Shamar Rinpoche was recognized by the 16th Gyalwa Karmapa in 1957 and was enthroned as the 14th Shamarpa in 1963. He was also recognized by the 14th Dalai Lama. Following many years of study with Buddhist scholars, he began in 1980 to spread the Buddha Dharma, teaching at Karma Kagyu centers throughout the world. Shamar Rinpoche was an accomplished Buddhist master and teacher, respected and cherished the world over.

In 1996, Shamar Rinpoche began organizing Bodhi Path Buddhist Centers, a network of centers covering many continents, in which a non-sectarian approach to meditation is practiced. In addition, he founded several nonprofit organizations throughout the world that are engaged in charitable activities, including projects to provide schooling for children born into poverty, to promote animal rights, and to provide medical care to women who would not otherwise have access to such care. Moreover, in addition to his teaching activities, he also published a number of books on Buddhism.

About the translator

Dr. Tina Draszczyk, M.A., studied Tibetology and Indology at the University of Hamburg. Since the early 1980s, she learned and practiced among others under the guidance of Shamar Rinpoche. Since the late 1980s, she repeatedly interpreted for him. From 1992 to 2005 she acted as an interpreter at the Karmapa International Buddhist Institute (KIBI) in New Delhi while continuing her own studies there at the same time. She completed her doctoral thesis at the Department for South Asian, Tibetan and Buddhist Studies of the University of Vienna on the integration of the notion of buddha nature in meditation practice. She has published a number of books on the interplay between Buddhist philosophy and meditation and teaches in Bodhi Path centers in Europe.

Publishing finished
in June 2023 by Pulsio
Publisher Number: 4025
Legal Deposit: June 2023
Printed in Bulgaria